ALABAMA

Sarah Tieck

Big Buddy BOOKS

Explore the

VISIT US AT
www.abdopublishing.com

Published by ABDO Publishing Company, PO Box 398166, Minneapolis, MN 55439.

Printed in the United States of America, North Mankato, Minnesota.
022012
092012

PRINTED ON RECYCLED PAPER

Coordinating Series Editor: Rochelle Baltzer
Contributing Editors: BreAnn Rumsch, Marcia Zappa
Graphic Design: Adam Craven
Cover Photograph: *Shutterstock*: Jeffrey M. Frank.
Interior Photographs/Illustrations: *Alamy*: © The Protected Art Archive (p. 17); *AP Photo*: AP Photo (pp. 13, 21, 25, 26), Copyright Bettmann/Corbis via AP Images (p. 23), Rob Carr (p. 21), Butch Dill (p. 27), North Wind Picture Archives via AP Images (p. 13); *iStockphoto*: ©iStockphoto.com/pelicankate (p. 27), ©iStockphoto.com/philipdyer (p. 9), ©iStockphoto.com/toddmedia (pp. 11, 29); *Shutterstock*: Florian Andronache (p. 30), Walter G Arce (p. 21), lloyd s clements (p. 5), Mike Flippo (p. 26), Jeffrey M. Frank (p. 5), Rob Hainer (p. 27), Phillip Lange (p. 30), Jason Patrick Ross (p. 30), Henryk Sadura (p. 9), SaraJo (p. 19), Mary Terriberry (p. 30), RadlovskYaroslav (p. 23).

All population figures taken from the 2010 US census.

Library of Congress Cataloging-in-Publication Data

Tieck, Sarah, 1976-
  Alabama / Sarah Tieck.
      p. cm. -- (Explore the United States)
  ISBN 978-1-61783-339-7
  1. Alabama--Juvenile literature. I. Title.
  F326.3.T54 2012
  976.1--dc23
                          2012000760

Contents

ONE NATION

The United States is a **diverse** country. It has farmland, cities, coasts, and mountains. Its people come from many different backgrounds. And, its history covers more than 200 years.

Today, the country includes 50 states. Alabama is one of these states. Let's learn more about Alabama and its story!

Did You Know?

Alabama became a state on December 14, 1819. It was the twenty-second state to join the nation.

Alabama's natural areas include thick forests and beautiful bays.

5

ALABAMA UP CLOSE

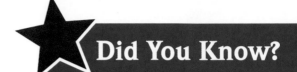
The United States has four main **regions**. Alabama is in the South.

Alabama has four states on its borders. Tennessee is north. Georgia is east, and Mississippi is west. Florida and the Gulf of Mexico are south.

Alabama has a total area of 51,701 square miles (133,905 sq km). About 4.8 million people live there.

REGIONS OF THE UNITED STATES

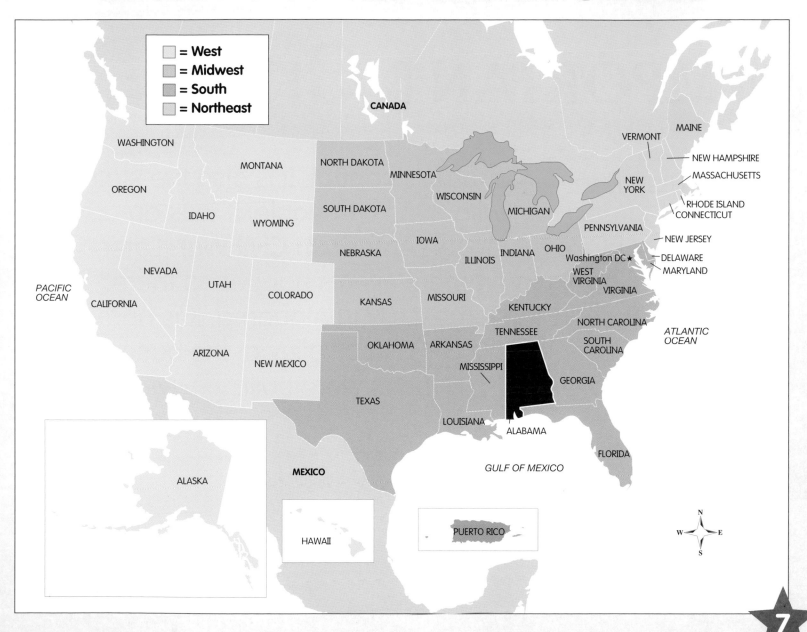

Legend:
- = West
- = Midwest
- = South
- = Northeast

CANADA

WASHINGTON

OREGON

IDAHO

MONTANA

NORTH DAKOTA

MINNESOTA

SOUTH DAKOTA

WISCONSIN

MICHIGAN

NEW YORK

VERMONT

MAINE

NEW HAMPSHIRE

MASSACHUSETTS

RHODE ISLAND
CONNECTICUT

PENNSYLVANIA

NEW JERSEY

WYOMING

NEBRASKA

IOWA

ILLINOIS

INDIANA

OHIO

Washington DC★

DELAWARE
MARYLAND

NEVADA

UTAH

COLORADO

KANSAS

MISSOURI

WEST
VIRGINIA

VIRGINIA

PACIFIC
OCEAN

CALIFORNIA

KENTUCKY

NORTH CAROLINA

TENNESSEE

SOUTH
CAROLINA

ATLANTIC
OCEAN

ARIZONA

NEW MEXICO

OKLAHOMA

ARKANSAS

MISSISSIPPI

TEXAS

LOUISIANA

ALABAMA

GEORGIA

FLORIDA

ALASKA

MEXICO

HAWAII

PUERTO RICO

GULF OF MEXICO

N
W E
S

7

Important Cities

Montgomery is Alabama's **capital**. It is also the state's second-largest city, with 205,764 people. It was an important place during the **American Civil War**. Later, many **civil rights movement** events happened there.

Birmingham is the largest city in Alabama. It is home to 212,237 people. This city is in a valley at the base of mountains. It grew as railroads were built.

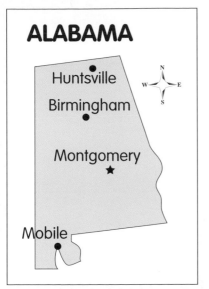

ALABAMA

- Huntsville
- Birmingham
- Montgomery ★
- Mobile

N W E S

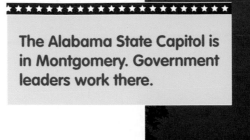

The Alabama State Capitol is in Montgomery. Government leaders work there.

Today, Birmingham is a leader in business in the South.

Mobile is one of the oldest US cities. It was founded by the French in 1702. This city is located on Mobile Bay. It is Alabama's only major city on a seaport. It is also the state's third-largest city, with 195,111 people.

Huntsville is another important city in Alabama. It is home to the US Space and Rocket Center. People call Huntsville "Rocket City, USA."

Many people visit the US Space and Rocket Center in Huntsville.

ALABAMA IN HISTORY

Alabama's history includes farming, war, and the **civil rights movement**. At first, much of Alabama was wild land. European settlers arrived and cleared land for farming. By the 1830s, cotton had become an important crop.

Slaves worked the cotton fields for landowners. After the **American Civil War**, they were freed. But by the 1950s, African Americans were still treated unfairly. The civil rights movement helped change this. Martin Luther King Jr. was one of the movement's leaders.

Slaves are people who are bought and sold as property. Many people were taken from Africa to work as slaves in the United States.

King gave speeches and led marches in Alabama.

13

Timeline

1819

Alabama became a state on December 14.

1838

Native Americans were forced to leave Alabama. This sad event was called the Trail of Tears.

1886

Montgomery's citywide electric trolley streetcars were the first in the United States.

1861

Alabama joined the Southern states to fight in the **American Civil War**.

1896

George Washington Carver began studying farming at a school in Tuskegee. His ideas about peanuts and sweet potatoes changed farming in the United States.

1800s

1915

Insects called boll weevils destroyed Alabama's cotton crop. Many families struggled to earn money. This changed the state's economy.

1960

The George C. Marshall Space Flight Center opened in Huntsville.

2005

Hurricane Katrina harmed Alabama's coast.

1900s

2000s

The Redstone Arsenal opened in Huntsville. There, rockets were made for the US government.

Martin Luther King Jr. and others said they would not use buses in Montgomery. This helped start the **civil rights movement**.

A set of tornadoes hit Alabama and several nearby states. It was the largest set ever recorded. At least 230 people in Alabama died.

1941

1955

2011

Across the Land

Alabama has forests, mountains, swamps, and beaches. The Mobile River is in southern Alabama. At Mobile Bay, it empties into the Gulf of Mexico.

Many types of animals make their homes in Alabama. Some of these include deer, owls, and hawks. Humpback whales are found off the coast in the Gulf of Mexico.

Did You Know?

Alabama's average summer temperature is 79°F (26°C). In the winter, the average is 48°F (9°C).

Swamps are wet areas where plants grow. Alligators, fish, frogs, birds, and mosquitoes often live in swamps.

17

Earning a Living

   For many years, Alabama was a farming state. Cotton was the most important crop. People even called it "King Cotton."

   Today, Alabama has farms that grow many crops. It is also a service and manufacturing state. It produces cars, paper, and foods. Many people also work in health care and **retail** jobs.

Corn (*above*), cotton, peanuts, and soybeans are some of Alabama's important crops.

Sports Page

Hank Aaron is one of Alabama's sports stars. Aaron was born in Mobile in 1934. He played Major League Baseball from 1954 to 1976. Aaron is one of baseball's best hitters of all time.

When many people think of Alabama, they think of NASCAR. That's because the state is home to the Talladega Superspeedway. It is the longest NASCAR track!

Did You Know?

NASCAR stands for the National Association for Stock Car Auto Racing.

Hank Aaron (*below*) broke records in baseball. Today, the Hank Aaron Stadium (*right*) stands in his honor in Mobile.

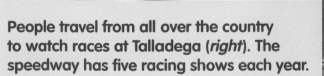

People travel from all over the country to watch races at Talladega (*right*). The speedway has five racing shows each year.

HOMETOWN HEROES

Many famous people have lived in Alabama. Helen Keller was born in Tuscumbia in 1880. Around 1882, she became deaf and blind after a sickness.

In 1887, Keller started working with a teacher named Anne Sullivan. Sullivan taught her to read and write. This changed Keller's life. She grew up to be a speaker and author.

Did You Know?

Harper Lee is another famous author from Alabama. She wrote the book *To Kill a Mockingbird*.

Sullivan (*right*) taught Keller (*left*) a word with a finger alphabet. Soon, Keller learned more words.

Today, Keller is pictured on Alabama's state quarter.

ALABAMA 1819
HELEN KELLER
SPIRIT OF COURAGE
2003
E PLURIBUS UNUM

Rosa Parks was born in Tuskegee in 1913. She became a **civil rights movement** leader. In 1955, Parks chose not to give up her bus seat to a white person. She was taken to jail for this. But, her choice helped change life for many Americans.

Paul William "Bear" Bryant was not born in Alabama. But, he was a famous University of Alabama football coach. From 1958 to 1982, he helped the Alabama Crimson Tide win many games. They won more games than any other major college football team in the 1960s and 1970s.

Parks helped spark the civil rights movement.

Bryant coached many great football players.

25

Tour Book

Do you want to go to Alabama? If you visit the state, here are some places to go and things to do!

 ## Taste

Try some southern food! Start the day with grits. Later, grab some fried chicken, sweet potatoes, and corn bread. For dessert, pecan pie is an Alabama favorite.

 ## Listen

WC Handy is a famous blues musician from Alabama. In the 1900s, he became known as the Father of the Blues. Today, the WC Handy Music Festival is held every July in Florence, Alabama.

 ★ Cheer

Catch a football game between University of Alabama and Auburn University. Both teams are known for playing well. They have been rivals for many years.

★ Remember

Visit historic ships and airplanes at Battleship Memorial Park in Mobile.

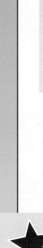

★ Discover

Learn about space travel at the US Space and Rocket Center in Huntsville. Some kids even attend space camp there!

A GREAT STATE

The story of Alabama is important to the United States. The people and places that make up this state offer something special to the country. Together with all the states, Alabama helps make the United States great.

Ships use Alabama's rivers to move goods from place to place.

Fast Facts

Date of Statehood:
December 14, 1819

Population (rank):
4,779,736
(23rd most-populated state)

Total Area (rank):
51,701 square miles
(30th largest state)

Motto:
"We Dare Defend Our Rights"

Nickname:
Cotton State,
Yellowhammer State

State Capital:
Montgomery

Flag:

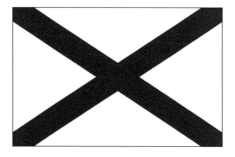

Flower: Common Camellia

Postal Abbreviation:
AL

Tree: Longleaf Pine

Bird: Yellowhammer

Important Words

American Civil War the war between the Northern and Southern states from 1861 to 1865.

capital a city where government leaders meet.

civil rights movement the public fight for civil rights for all citizens. Civil rights include the right to vote and freedom of speech.

diverse made up of things that are different from each other.

region a large part of a country that is different from other parts.

retail the business of selling goods to people who will use them.

Web Sites

To learn more about Alabama, visit ABDO Publishing Company online. Web sites about Alabama are featured on our Book Links page. These links are routinely monitored and updated to provide the most current information available.

www.abdopublishing.com

Index